How Did We Find Out About
COMETS?

Isaac Asimov

Illustrated by David Wool

D0061961

AN AVON CAMELOT BOOK

AVON BOOKS
A division of
The Hearst Corporation
1790 Broadway
New York, New York 10019

First Camelot Printing, February 1981

CAMELOT TRADEMARK REG. U.S. PAT. OFF. AND IN
OTHER COUNTRIES, MARCA REGISTRADA, HECHO EN U.S.A.

Printed in the U.S.A.

10 9 8 7 6 5 4 3 2

How Did We Find Out
About
COMETS?

ISAAC ASIMOV is a distinguished scientist as well as America's foremost writer on science for both adults and young readers. Born in Russia, Mr. Asimov came to this country with his parents at the age of three, and grew up in Brooklyn. He has written over two hundred books, and his instincts for probing the unknown and his warm understanding of human nature draw millions of readers—young and old—to his writings.

DAVID WOOL is a well-known commercial artist and industrial designer. His interests range from raising cats to studying history and archaeology.

How Did We Find Out About
About
COMETS?

To Ken Franklin and George Hamilton,
who bring astronomy to the people

Contents

1 The Hairy Stars

HUMAN BEINGS HAVE BEEN watching the sky at night for many thousands of years because it is so beautiful.

For one thing, there are thousands of stars scattered over the sky, some brighter than others. These stars make a pattern that is the same night after night and that slowly turns in a smooth and regular way.

There is the moon, which does not seem a mere dot of light like the stars, but a larger body. Sometimes it is a perfect circle of light but at other times it is a different shape—a half-circle or a curved crescent. It moves against the stars from night to night. One midnight, it could be near a particular star, and the next midnight, quite far away from that star.

There are also visible five starlike objects that are brighter than the stars. We call them Mercury, Venus,

Mars, Jupiter and Saturn. They, too, move against the stars from night to night.

The ancients called these five bright objects "planets," from a Greek word meaning "wandering," because they wander across the sky. The moon was also considered a planet and so was the sun which shone in the daytime. There were believed to be seven planets altogether.

The ancients studied the sky night after night, and they saw that the planets moved in a regular fashion. The moon moved in a circular path around the sky. It would start out near one star, make a complete circle, and come back to that same star after a little more than 27 days.

It could all be predicted. The moon repeated its path over and over again, and the ancients who watched the stars ("astronomers") could tell in advance just where the moon would be on a certain day in the future and what its shape would be.

The other planets had more complicated paths. Sometimes they would move in the same direction as the moon, but occasionally each one would turn and move in the opposite direction for a while. They moved at different speeds, and all moved more slowly than the moon.

Just the same, if the planets were watched over a period of time, a pattern could be seen. After a while, you could predict how each planet was going to move and where it would be.

Even very unusual events such as an eclipse of the sun or of the moon could be predicted. An eclipse of

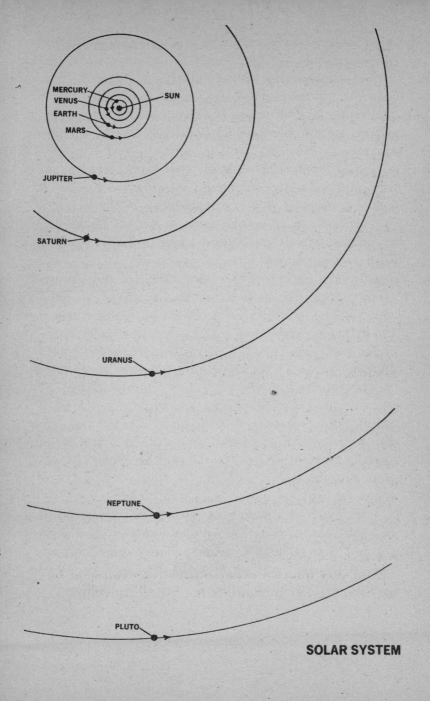

SOLAR SYSTEM

the sun took place when the moon moved in front of it. Astronomers learned to tell in advance when that would happen. An eclipse of the moon took place when the moon and the sun were on opposite sides of the earth and the earth's shadow fell on the moon. Three thousand years ago, eclipses could be predicted.

It was comforting to know that each planet in the sky followed a particular path over and over again. It seemed to show that the machinery of the universe was working in an orderly way. And if the machinery was working well in the skies, it was probably working well on earth, too.

But what happened if, every once in a while, something unusual happened in the sky? What if something happened that was so out of the ordinary that it could not be predicted? Might that not mean something had gone wrong with the machinery? Might that not mean something unusual was going to happen on the earth, too?

As it happened, every once in a while, a new kind of shining object appeared in the night sky; one that was like nothing else you could see in the sky. It was not just a point of light like the stars or the planets. It was not a bright circle of light like the sun or the full moon.

It was something that was larger than a star but it did not have sharp outlines. It was like a patch of shining fog, and out of one side of it there came a long, curved streamer of foggy light that grew fainter and fainter as it stretched outward.

DIAGRAM OF COMET

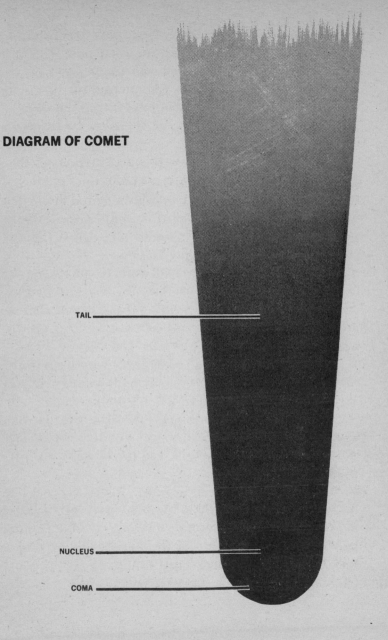

TAIL

NUCLEUS

COMA

It was as though it were a fuzzy star, with shining hair streaming out of it. The ancient Greeks called it "aster kometes" which, in their language, means "hairy star." We keep the second part of the Greek name and call such an object in the sky a "comet."

At the center of the comet, there is sometimes a bright starlike dot called a "nucleus." The hazy light around the nucleus is the "coma" (KOH-muh). The long trail of hazy light from one side is the "tail."

The ancient astronomers could not predict when a comet would come, or where it would appear. They could not tell what path it would take across the sky, or when and where it would disappear.

Even after astronomers had worked out the movement of all the other objects in the sky and had explained eclipses, they were still puzzled about comets. A comet just came, traveled across the sky, and disappeared.

The more people came to expect everything in the sky to follow a regular path, the more frightened they became of comets. Maybe, when a comet came crashing into the smooth workings of the sky, it meant that some disaster would take place on earth. Some important person might die; there might be a war or a plague.

Whenever a comet did appear, there was sure to be something catastrophic happening on earth (after all, there always is.) People would say that the comet had served as a warning of this event. Then the next time a comet appeared, they would be all the more frightened.

For instance, there was a comet in the sky in 44 B.C. which was the same year that the great Roman dictator, Julius Caesar, was assassinated. There was also a comet in the sky in 1066 A.D. which was the year that William of Normandy invaded England and conquered it. That was a disaster to the English, although the comet was lucky for William.

HALLEY'S COMET OF 1066 AS ILLUSTRATED ON BAYEUX TAPESTRY (11TH CENTURY)

People who don't really understand what is going on in the sky are frightened by comets even today. They think a comet will bring disaster or that it means the end of the world is coming.

Actually, comets are no more than objects in the sky. They have no effect at all on the earth, one way or the other. But as long as people do not know what comets are, or where they come from, or where they go, or what makes them appear in the sky, they will worry about them.

Fortunately, astronomers have learned, little by little, the answer to these questions about comets, and educated people are no longer afraid of them.

2 Distance and Orbits

THE FIRST PERSON to consider comets thoughtfully was a Greek philosopher named Aristotle (AR-is-TOT-ul) who lived more than 2,000 years ago. About 350 B.C., he decided that since all the objects in the sky moved in regular paths, comets, because of their irregular behavior, could not be objects in the sky. He felt that comets were patches of air that somehow caught fire. Such patches of burning air would move slowly through the air and finally burn out. When that happened, the comet would disappear.

Aristotle was considered the greatest thinker of ancient times. His ideas were taken very seriously. For about 1,800 years, astronomers agreed with Aristotle and believed that comets were not heavenly bodies, but burning patches of air.

ARISTOTLE

One of the reasons why no better explanation was suggested for a long time was that after the time of the ancient Greeks, comets became so frightening that no one really wanted to look at them carefully. It wasn't until 1473 that a German astronomer, Regiomontanus (ree-jee-oh-mon-TAY-nus), observed a comet and put down its position in the sky night after night. His work was the beginning of the modern study of comets.

When a comet appeared in 1532, two astronomers studied it and noticed something interesting. One astronomer was an Italian named Girolamo Fracastoro (fra-kas-TOH-roh) and the other was an Austrian named Peter Apian (AY-pee-an). Both of them noticed that the tail of the comet always pointed away from the sun. When the comet moved past the sun from one side to the other, the tail changed direction.

This was the first important scientific discovery about comets, and it has turned out to be true of all comets. Every comet that astronomers have studied has had a tail pointing away from the sun. This meant there had to be some connection between comets and the sun.

Then, in 1577, there was an even more astonishing discovery. In that year, a comet appeared in the sky and it was studied by a Danish astronomer, Tycho Brahe, who is usually known by his first name, Tycho (TY-koh). Tycho not only decided to take note of the comet's position in the sky, but he also thought he would try to find out how far away it was.

One way of finding out the distance of something in the sky is to make use of "parallax" (PA-ra-laks). To do this you must look at an object from two different places and note the way the object seems to change position.

You can see how this works if you hold your finger in front of your face, close your left eye, and look at it with your right eye. You will see that it is near a particular part of the background. Keep the finger and your head in the same place, and close your right eye. Now look at the finger with your left eye and you will see that the finger has shifted position against the background.

The amount of shift depends on how far away the finger is from your eyes. (Try it and see for yourself.) The farther away the finger is from your eyes, the smaller the shift, or parallax. For something very far away from your eyes, you cannot see any shift at all.

To see the parallax of something very far away you have to look at it first from one place, then from another place a distance away (for example, a mile).

If something is as far away as the moon, even a mile change in position might not be enough. But what about a change in position of a few hundred miles? You might then see a small shift in the position of the moon against the background of stars. From the amount of the parallax and from the distance between the two viewing places, the distance to the moon can be calculated.

This was done by the ancient Greek astronomers. As long ago as 130 B.C., one of them, Hipparchus

PARALLAX

(hih-PAHR-kus), had calculated that the moon was about 240,000 miles from the earth.

In 1577, Tycho decided to try to measure the parallax of the comet in the sky, as Hipparchus had measured the parallax of the moon. If the comet were part of the air, it should be much closer than the moon, and it should have a bigger parallax.

Tycho arranged to have an astronomer in Germany, a few hundred miles away, note the position of the comet against the stars at a certain hour of a particular night. Another astronomer observed it at exactly the same time from Bohemia, while Tycho himself noted the position at the same time from his own observatory in Denmark.

Tycho studied the results and found that the comet appeared to be in just about the same place compared to the stars no matter where the observer was standing. There was hardly any shift. The parallax was much smaller than that of the moon.

This meant that the comet had to be farther away than the moon. In fact, Tycho decided the comet had to be at least four times as far away as the moon—it was, therefore, about a million miles away.

This figure was not accurate. Actually, the comet was much farther away than that. But Tycho's result was still important. It showed that the comet could not be a burning patch of air, and that Aristotle's theory was wrong. The comet was a heavenly body, just as the planets were.

If comets were heavenly bodies, why did they look and act so differently from other heavenly bodies?

NICHOLAS COPERNICUS

Tycho could not say, but in his time, astronomers were beginning to take a new look at the universe.

Until then, astronomers had thought that the various planets moved in circles around the earth. In 1543, however, a Polish astronomer, Nicholas Copernicus (koh-PER-nih-kus), showed that it made more sense to look at things in another way.

He said that only the moon moved in a circle around the earth. The earth itself moved in a circle around the sun. All the other planets also moved in circles around the sun. If astronomers accepted this, it became much easier to figure out the motions of the planets. (The path followed by a body moving around another body is called an "orbit," from a Latin word meaning "circle.")

The sun and all the objects that moved around it make up the "solar system" (so called because in Latin the sun is called "sol").

A German astronomer, Johannes Kepler (KEP-ler), who had been one of Tycho's assistants, disagreed with part of Copernicus's theory. After studying the motions of the planets in the sky, Kepler said, in 1609, that the planets moved around the sun in orbits that were not circles. Each planet moved around the sun in an "ellipse."

An ellipse looks like a flattened circle. It can be so slightly flattened that you cannot tell it from a circle. It can be more flattened so that you can see at a glance that it is not a circle. Or it can be very flattened so that it looks long and thin, something like a cigar.

The orbit of the earth around the sun is an ellipse

JOHANNES KEPLER

that is only very slightly flattened. It is almost circular. The moon's orbit around the earth is more flattened, and Mercury's orbit around the sun is still more flattened. Even Mercury's orbit, which is more flattened than that of any other planet known in Kepler's time, is not *very* flattened. Its orbit still looks like that of a circle.

The sun is not at the very center of the elliptical orbits of the planets around it. The flatter the ellipse, the closer one end of it is to the sun.

When the earth moves around the sun, it is only 91,500,000 miles from the sun at one end of its orbit, but 94,500,000 miles from the sun at the other end. The farther distance is less than four percent greater than the nearer distance.

Mercury's orbit around the sun is more elliptical, so there is a bigger difference. When Mercury is at the end of the ellipse nearer the sun, it is only 28,000,000 miles away. At the other end, it is 44,000,000 miles from the sun. The farther distance is about 50 percent greater than the nearer distance.

Kepler was able to work out elliptical orbits for all the planets, but what about the comets? If they were heavenly bodies, did that mean they had orbits, too?

Kepler carefully studied the reports he had about the changing positions of comets in the sky. Finally, he decided that comets must move in straight lines. He thought they came from far out in space, passed near the sun, then traveled onward far out in space in the other direction.

They could only be seen when they were close to

the sun and reflected its light. Before they came close enough to the sun, they could not be seen. After they moved far enough from the sun, they again could not be seen. According to Kepler's view, comets were not part of the solar system. Each comet just passed through the solar system once and was never seen again.

An Italian astronomer, Giovanni Alfonso Borelli (boh-REL-lee), carefully studied the positions of a comet that appeared in the sky in 1664. He found he had to disagree with Kepler.

The only way to make sense out of the path the comet took across the sky, Borelli said, was to suppose that it changed direction as it passed the sun. It came

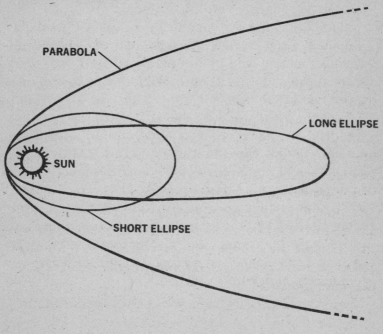

closer and closer to the sun, along a line that was nearly straight. Then it moved around the sun, and left it along a line that was again nearly straight but had changed direction.

The way Borelli explained this was to point out that ellipses could be very flattened indeed. They could be so flattened that they would resemble a very long thin cigar. In fact, if you imagined an ellipse that was more and more flattened, and longer and longer, you could eventually imagine one that was so flattened it just went on and on forever. Such an ellipse would be closed only at one end. In the other direction, it would never be closed, but would just go on and on. A one-ended ellipse that goes on and on forever is called a "parabola" (pa-RA-boh-luh).

Borelli decided that a comet's orbit was a parabola, with the sun very near the closed end. The comet came in at one side of the parabola, went whizzing around the sun, and then moved outward along the other side of the parabola.

Borelli's view was like that of Kepler, except that the orbit he conceived was not a straight line. Like Kepler, Borelli thought comet was originally so far away it could not be seen. As it came closer and closer to the sun, it grew bright enough to be seen, and then as it went farther and farther from the sun, it once more became too dim to be seen. In Borelli's view, as in Kepler's, the comets were not members of the solar system. Each comet just passed through the solar system once and never returned.

3 The Comet That Returned

KEPLER'S NOTION of elliptical orbits worked very well for the planets, but there were lots of questions left. Why did the planets go around the sun in ellipses instead of circles (or some other curve)? Why did planets move faster when they were nearer the sun than when they were farther away?

These questions and many others were answered by the English scientist Isaac Newton. In 1687, he published a book in which he described his "Theory of Universal Gravitation." According to this theory, every body in the universe attracted every other body. The strength of the attraction between two particular bodies depended on the "mass" of each body (how much matter it contained) and on how far apart the two bodies were. The strength of the attraction could

SIR ISAAC NEWTON

be calculated by a simple mathematical equation.

Newton showed how to use the equation to work out the exact orbit of the moon around the earth and of the planets around the sun.

The same equation explained why each planet moved quickly at times and slowly at other times, and why some planets moved faster than others. It explained little changes in the motion of the planets that were produced by the tiny pulls of one planet on another even as all were caught in the gigantic pull of the much larger sun. It explained the tides on the earth and many other things, too.

But comets were the one set of heavenly bodies that remained puzzling. If comets traveled in orbits that were parabolas, Newton's theory could account for that fact. Suppose, though, the orbits were not quite parabolas. Suppose the orbits were just very long ellipses and were closed at the other end.

We can only observe the comet at the end of the orbit near the sun. The shape of that small part of the enormous orbit would be a narrow curve if the ellipse were very long. The shape would be slightly wider, if the ellipse were even longer, and still wider if the ellipse never closed at all and were a parabola.

The differences in the shapes of the small bit of orbit we could see, as predicted by Newton's theory, were so tiny that astronomers in Newton's time could not tell them apart. They couldn't really say whether the orbit of a comet was a very long ellipse or whether it was a parabola.

It made a difference. If a comet's orbit were a parabola, it would visit the solar system once and would never be seen again. If the orbit were a very, very long ellipse, then eventually the comet would come to the other end of the ellipse, turn around and begin to approach the sun again. The comet would return.

In fact, if astronomers could calculate the exact length of the orbit, they could even predict *when* the comet would return. That would be a big victory for Newton's theory.

Newton had a young friend, Edmund Halley (HAL-ee), who had helped Newton publish his book and who was interested in the comet problem.

In 1682, a comet appeared and Halley had very carefully studied its positions and the way it moved across the sky. From the part of the orbit he could see, he couldn't tell whether it would ever return.

It seemed to him, though, that if a comet did return it should do so at regular periods—every so many years—and that it should always trace the same curve across the sky. He therefore began to collect all the reports on the positions of earlier comets that he could find. By 1705, he had collected good reports on two dozen comets of the past, and began to compare them.

He noticed that the comet of 1682, which he had himself observed, followed the same curve across the sky that the comet of 1607 had. The same curve had also been followed by the comet of 1532 (which Fracastoro and Apian had studied) and the comet of 1456.

These comets had come at 75 or 76 year periods. Could it be that it was a single comet that returned

**HALLEY'S COMET
OVER PARIS 1910**

every 75 years or so? Could it be that it was a "periodic comet"?

Halley worked out the orbit for a comet that returned every 75 years and followed the same curve in the sky that the comet of 1682 had followed.

The results were quite amazing. Saturn, the planet farthest from the sun (as far as was known in Halley's time) was never farther from the sun than 930,000,000 miles. The comet of 1682, however, moved out as far as 3,200,000,000 miles from the sun before it reached the other end of its elliptical orbit and began moving inward again. The comet moved over three times as far away from the sun as Saturn ever moved.

On the other hand, when the comet passed along the end of the ellipse that was near the sun, it came as close as 54,000,000 miles from the sun. This was only about half of earth's distance from the sun.

After Halley had calculated the orbit, he announced that the comet of 1682 would return some time in 1758 and would follow a particular path across the sky.

Halley did not live long enough to see the comet's return. He was 86 years old when he died in 1742, but that was much too soon to see the return.

There were, however, others who were watching for it. A French astronomer, Alexis Claude Clairault (klay-ROH) considered the orbit as outlined by Halley. He realized that the gravitational pull of the large planets, Jupiter and Saturn, would delay the comet a little bit. It would not pass around the sun till some time in 1759.

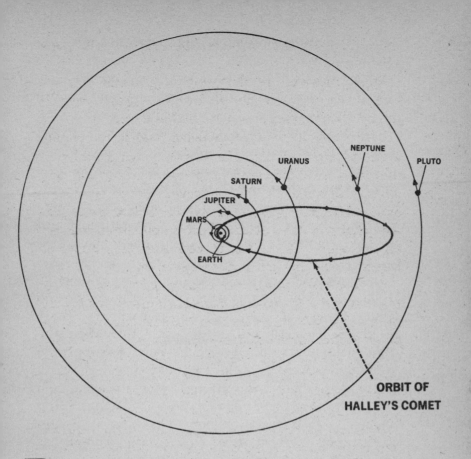

URANUS · NEPTUNE · PLUTO · SATURN · JUPITER · MARS · EARTH

ORBIT OF
HALLEY'S COMET

In 1758, astronomers eagerly watched that part of
the sky in which Halley had said the comet should appear. They did not have to depend only on their eyes
as Tycho and earlier astronomers had done. The telescope had been invented in 1609.

On December 25, 1758, Christmas Day, a German
farmer named Johann Georg Palitzch (PA-lich), who

was an amateur astronomer, spotted the comet. The comet of 1682 had appeared in the sky where Halley said it would and proceeded to move along the path Halley had predicted for it. It moved around the sun quite close to the time Clairault had predicted.

There was no question that it was the comet of 1682 and that it had returned. That meant that some of the mystery of comets was cleared up. They followed the same rules as the other bodies of the solar system except that their orbits were more elliptical.

Naturally, the comet of 1682 that returned and passed around the sun in 1759 came to be called "Halley's comet."

Halley's comet is the most famous comet there is. It happens to be the one which was in the sky in 1066 when William of Normandy was preparing to invade England. It was also in the sky in 11 B.C. about the time when Jesus may have been born. Some people think it may have been the "Star of Bethlehem."

Halley's comet has returned twice since Palitzch saw it. It came back in 1835 and was glowing in the sky when Mark Twain was born. Then it came back in 1910 and Mark Twain died when it was glowing in the sky. It will come back yet again in 1985-1986.

It is fortunate that Halley's comet has an orbit that is short enough for it to come back every 75 years or so. What if its orbit were longer? It might then take many hundreds, or even thousands, of years to return.

Some comets appeared in the 1800s—in 1812, in 1861, in 1882—that were very large and bright. They seem to have orbits that are so long that they may take

COMET OVER LONDON 1858

many thousands of years to return. The last time they were near the sun, human beings were just primitive cavemen who did not think much about comets. When they come back again, who knows what the world and its people will be like!

The orbits of such comets cannot be calculated from the little part of the orbit we see. Since they have made no previous returns when there were astronomers watching the sky, we cannot compare orbits, as Halley did for the orbits of the comet of 1682.

Halley's comet has a shorter orbit than any other bright comet in existence and it is the only bright one whose orbit is known and whose returns can be surely predicted.

Just the same, astronomers now know that comets are members of the solar system, and have orbits that are elliptical and can be calculated if only we can see enough of them.

4 Faint Comets

HALLEY'S PREDICTION of the return of the comet of 1682 and its actual return on schedule in 1759 made astronomers begin to pay more attention to comets. They did not have to wait for bright comets, which might not appear for long periods of time. With their telescopes they could locate many comets too faint to see with the naked eye.

Many faint comets were found. In fact, every year a few were discovered.

In 1770, a Swedish astronomer named Anders Jean Lexell discovered a comet. He followed its path as it traveled and found that its orbit was easy to calculate. It moved in an ellipse that was much shorter than that of Halley's comet. In fact, its orbit would bring it to the neighborhood of the sun every 5.5 years.

In that case, why was it that it had never been seen before? No comet had ever been seen passing along the sky on the route Lexell's comet had taken.

Lexell traced the path of the comet back into space to see where it had been before he first saw it. He found that it must have passed near Jupiter. It passed so close to Jupiter that it must have moved among the planet's four large satellites.

Lexell decided that the comet had had a long elliptical orbit to begin with, which was why it had not been seen before. When it passed close to Jupiter, however, the gravitational pull of that large planet made the comet curve out of its path. It took up a new orbit in an ellipse that was much shorter than the old one.

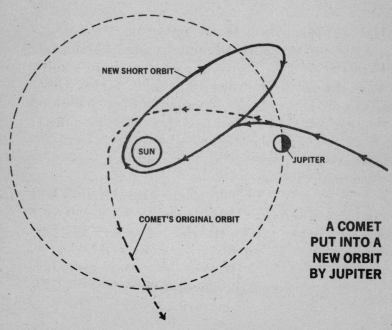

NEW SHORT ORBIT

SUN

JUPITER

COMET'S ORIGINAL ORBIT

A COMET
PUT INTO A
NEW ORBIT
BY JUPITER

However, the new short orbit did not stay put, either. Lexell's comet never appeared again. There was more calculation and it seemed that, on its path away from the sun after its 1770 approach, the comet once again passed close to Jupiter. Once again it curved out of its orbit.

This time it took up an orbit that was spread out so widely that it did not close at the other end. It spread out even more widely than a parabola would. The curve of the new orbit was a hyperbola (hy-PUR-boh-luh).

Jupiter had hurled Lexell's comet out of the solar system altogether. Every once in a while a comet is lost in this fashion.

What happened to Lexell's comet also showed how carefully one had to calculate a comet's orbit. An orbit could always be changed by the various planets.

Most important of all was the fact that Lexell's comet passed very close to Jupiter and its satellites and yet produced no changes in *their* orbits. Lexell's comet must have had so little mass that it had almost no gravitational pull.

Until then, it had been thought that comets might be large, very dangerous bodies that could destroy the earth by colliding with it.

Now astronomers knew they were actually tiny bodies. They might be surrounded by comas that took up a great deal of room, and they might have tails that were many millions of miles long. However, the amount of actual matter, or "mass", in the coma and the tail was very small indeed. And it was the mass that counted.

The comets were the first really small bodies discovered in the solar system.

In one particular way, astronomers of the 1700s were disappointed in comets. After Halley had worked out the orbit of Halley's comet, there had been the feeling that many orbits might be worked out—but for a hundred years after Halley's time, no other comet had its orbit worked out. For a while, Lexell had thought he had one, but that orbit changed.

Then, in 1818, a French astronomer, Jean Louis Pons, found a comet he thought was new. A German astronomer, Johann Franz Encke (ENK-uh), studied its path and found that several earlier comets had followed the same path. There were comets in 1786, 1795, and 1805 that did.

With this information, Encke calculated the orbit of the comet and found its ellipse was so short that it returned to the neighborhood of the sun every 3.3 years. The ellipse was so short that it didn't even extend outward as far as Jupiter's orbit.

The comet came to be known as "Encke's comet." It was the first comet after Halley's comet to have its orbit worked out and to actually follow that orbit and return when it was supposed to.

Encke's comet is a "short-period comet." Though many comets have had their orbits worked out since Encke's time, no other comet has been found to have an orbit so short, or to come back to the neighborhood of the sun so often. Altogether, Encke's comet has been observed by astronomers on nearly 50 returns to the sun.

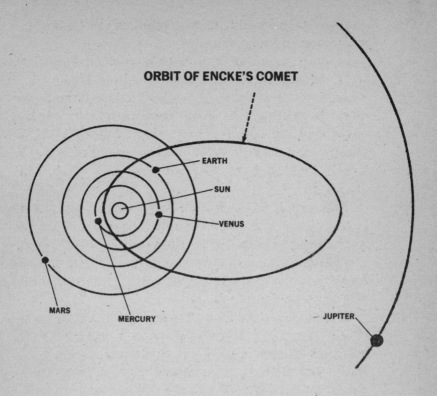

ORBIT OF ENCKE'S COMET

EARTH

SUN

VENUS

MARS

MERCURY

JUPITER

Encke's comet can only be seen through a telescope since it is very dim. Even in a telescope one can only see a small coma around it, and there is never any tail.

In fact, all the short-period comets—those that return to the neighborhood of the sun every few years— are faint. The coma that is formed each time is blown away into the tail and never comes back. Each time the comet returns, there is less material in it to form a coma and tail.

This means that a comet must get less bright at each return and slowly fade away. Comets that have small orbits and return frequently to the sun have faded away long ago. Only comets with long orbits that return to the neighborhood of the sun once in a long while are still bright when they return.

5 The Comet That Died

WHAT HAPPENS TO A COMET as it fades? Judging from Encke's comet, it might be that a small stony nucleus remains behind.

But is this so every time? Is there always a stony nucleus that remains behind? The answer to that was discovered in the 1800s.

In 1826, an Australian astronomer, Wilhelm von Biela (BEE-luh), sighted a comet. He studied its position night after night. From the path it followed across the sky, he decided that its orbit was a short ellipse. It was not as short as the ellipse of Encke's comet, though.

He calculated that the comet came back to the vicinity of the sun every 6.8 years. Working backward, this meant that the comet had been seen on a number of its earlier visits. In fact, a comet that had been sighted in 1772 must have been the same as the one now called "Biela's comet."

Biela's comet was the second short-period comet to have its orbit worked out. It began to return on schedule, just as Encke's comet was doing.

In fact, one astronomer went over Biela's figures and calculated that Biela's comet would make its closest approach to the sun on November 27, 1832. He was right to the very day.

After that, Biela's comet came back again in 1839. In that year, however, the position of the earth and of Biela's comet were such that the comet would always appear to be very near the sun. It was too faint to be seen under those conditions.

Astronomers were not concerned, however. They were sure it would come back once again in February 1846, when it would be easy to see. So they waited.

In December 1845, Biela's comet was sighted by the waiting astronomers. It was coming back right on schedule.

But it was not a normal appearance. An American scientist, Matthew Fontaine Maury, pointed out that there was a second, fainter comet accompanying Biela's comet. The two comets moved in step as they traveled toward the sun. What had happened?

Perhaps during the 1839 approach to the sun when the comet could not be seen, enough of its matter had been heated and pulled out of it to leave behind a dumbbell shape. And that "dumbbell" had broken in two, so there were two comets where there had been one before.

What would happen at the next approach to the sun

BIELA'S COMET

in 1852? The comet was then seen by an Italian astronomer, Pietro Angelo Secchi (SEK-kee). There were still two comets, but now they were separated by quite a distance. The pull of nearby planets must have affected each of them a little differently, so their orbits were no longer quite the same. Secchi's measurements showed the two comets to be 1,500,000 miles apart.

The next return was to be in 1859, but this time it would again be in the sky only at twilight and would not be seen. Astronomers would have to wait until 1866, at which time it should be easily visible.

It was not. The year 1866 came and went and there was no sign of either part of Biela's comet. Furthermore, it has never been seen again. It was gone. And Jupiter had not been in a position to pull it into a new orbit.

Could it be that in the 1859 return, what was left of the material of the comet had been turned into a coma and tail, and now all was gone?

Nothing like that happened to Encke's comet. Perhaps that was because Encke's comet had a rocky core and Biela's comet had not.

But was there really nothing at all left of Biela's comet? That question brings us to something else: every once in a while there is a "shooting star" or "meteor" in the sky. It is not a real star, of course. It is just a little bit of matter that has been moving through space and has collided with the earth.

As the bit of matter moves through the atmosphere at great speed, it heats up because of friction with the

THE WILLAMETTE METEOR

air. It gets hot enough to glow and then you see it like a shining line of light that appears and then quickly comes to an end. Sometimes, the piece of matter heating up in air is so large that not all of it melts and burns away. What remains hits the ground as a lump of stone or iron that is called a "meteorite." Such meteorites are very rare.

Most meteors are very small objects in the air, objects far too small to end up as meteorites. They may be no larger than the head of a pin. Even such tiny objects can glow and appear as streaks of light.

These tiny meteors are very common. Sometimes, in fact, the earth seems to pass through a whole cloud of such tiny pinhead bodies. In that case, there is a "meteor shower."

A particularly remarkable meteor shower was seen from the United States in 1833. The sky was alive with lines of light, seeming to fall as thickly as snowflakes. Some people who were watching thought that all the stars were falling from the sky and that it was the end of the world. But after the meteor shower ended, all the stars were still in the sky.

These small bodies burn up completely in the air. No matter how thick a meteor shower is, nothing ever reaches the ground.

The meteor shower of 1833 made astronomers wonder about such clouds of particles that the earth passed through every once in a while. Could it be that they moved around the sun in a regular orbit?

The Italian astronomer, Giovanni Virginio Schiaparelli (skyah-pah-REL-lee), considered the matter.

FANTASTIC METEOR SHOWER OF NOVEMBER 12, 1833

He gathered all the material he could find about when meteor showers appeared and from what part of the sky they seemed to come. His calculations in the 1860s showed that clouds of meteors moved about the sun in orbits that were long ellipses. Their orbits resembled those of comets. Could it be that there was some connection between those meteor clouds and comets?

Schiaparelli thought so. There was one meteor shower that usually appeared in August and seemed to come out of a spot in the constellation Perseus. These meteors were therefore called "Perseids" (PER-see-idz). Schiaparelli showed that the Perseids moved in the same orbit as "Tuttle's comet." (This comet had been discovered in 1853 by the American astronomer Charles Wesley Tuttle. It returned to the vicinity of the sun every 14 years.)

It began to look as though a comet might be made up of material that would evaporate and become a gas in the heat of the sun. Scattered through this gaseous material were fine bits of rock. When the gaseous material evaporated, fine bits of rock were left which glittered in the sun. It was these that could be seen in the coma and the tail.

Perhaps it was these fine bits of rock from heated comets that produced the meteors in the earth's atmosphere. Every time a comet passed near the sun, meteor bits left it and then moved about the sun on their own. Gradually, they spread out through the entire orbit of the comet. There were usually more bits near the comet than far away from it.

Eventually, if the comet had no rocky core, all of it would turn into a cloud of particles. Could it be that this was what had happened to Biela's comet?

After Schiaparelli had shown that the Perseids were produced by Tuttle's comet, astronomers applied this knowledge to Biela's comet. They knew what the orbit of Biela's comet was and they expected there would be meteors all along it. There would be a particularly thick cluster of them in the spot where the comet itself would have been.

They waited for the time when the earth would be near that spot. One astronomer, E. Weiss, predicted that there would be a meteor shower on November 28, 1872. He was wrong by just one day; it appeared on November 27.

This particular meteor shower was called the 'Bielids.'' It appeared several more times and then faded out. The particle cloud spread through the orbit but was not thick enough anywhere to make a good shower.

6 What Comets Are

IN 1950, THE DUTCH astronomer Jan Hendrik Oort (AWRT) suggested that there was a belt of small bodies far out from the sun. They might be as much as several thousand billion miles away, so no one could possibly see them out there even with the biggest telescope. There might be as many as a hundred billion of them in that distant belt. *These small bodies become comets when they come closer to the sun.*

The American astronomer Fred Lawrence Whipple suggested that it was so cold far out there that the distant comets were made up chiefly of materials that would be gases on earth. Such gases as "ammonia," "methane," "cyanogen" would all be solid, icelike substances making up the comets. There would also be ordinary ice or frozen water in the comets.

In among all this icy material there would be a fine scattering of rocky particles. At the center, there might be a rocky core, or there might not.

Every once in a while, one of these far-distant comets might be slowed up as it made its huge circle about the sun. This loss of speed might be caused by a collision between two of them, or because of the pull of a distant star.

The slowed comet would then drop in toward the sun in a new orbit that would be a very long ellipse. It would pass near the planets, and if it came near enough to the sun, it would shine brightly enough for us to see it. Then it would pass around the sun and head back to the far distances. In its new orbit it might come close to the sun only once every million years or so.

When a comet approaches the sun in this way, the icy materials it is composed of would evaporate. The rocky particles would be freed and would form the coma.

In 1958, the American scientist Eugene Norman Parker showed that tiny particles, even smaller than atoms, were always hurtling out of the sun at great speeds in all directions. These particles form the "solar wind." It is this solar wind that strikes the coma of the comet and drives it away from the sun to form a tail.

Comets which are entering the neighborhood of the sun for the first time can produce a huge coma that may take up more space than the sun itself, and a long tail that may stretch for hundreds of millions of miles.

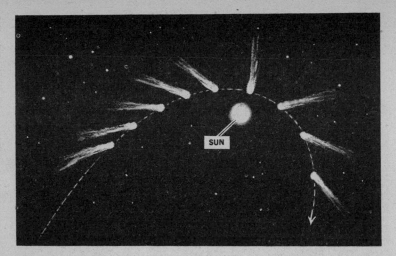

ACTION OF SOLAR WIND ON COMET'S TAIL

Every once in a while, such a comet is curved out of its orbit by a planet, usually by Jupiter, the largest of the planets. It then can move along a shorter elliptical orbit. It loses so much of its material as it passes the sun many times that it quickly grows faint. Even Halley's comet is growing fainter.

A comet that came from the far outer reaches of space, perhaps for the first time, and was very bright, was seen in 1882.

Scientists have been waiting ever since 1882 for a new comet from the outer reaches to arrive so that they could study it with the new instruments and new knowledge they have developed in the last century. Finally, in 1973, a Czech astronomer, Lubos Kohoutek (koh-HOH-tek), sighted a comet quite a long distance from the earth. That meant it had to be a large

Six views of Comet Kohoutek as seen by the astronauts aboard Skylab at the time the comet passed closest to the sun

1 December 18, 1973

2 December 29, 1973

3 December 30, 1973

4 December 31, 1973

5 January 2, 1974   **6 January 5, 1974**

one or it would not reflect enough light to be seen.

From its orbit, "Comet Kohoutek" or "Kohoutek's comet" seemed to be arriving from the far-distant belt of small bodies. It made its closest approach to the sun on December 28, 1973, the very day on which I am writing this. It didn't become as bright as astronomers hoped it might; but it has been studied by men in space on the Skylab statellite, and it will be studied further as it moves outward from the sun again.

Perhaps some day in the future, when once again a new comet arrives from far-distant space, astronomers will be on a rocket ship ready to land on it.

Then, instead of being afraid of a comet as a sign of bad luck, men will be touching it and bringing back to earth pieces of it for close study.

61

FUTURE SPACE PROBE APPROACHING COMET

Index